PEACE
in a FLAMING
STORM

PEACE
in a FLAMING
STORM

A 31 Day Journey
Turning the Scars of Life Into the Joy of Christ

Wendi Sue Catton

Pleasant W●rd

Packaged by Pleasant Word, PO Box 428, Enumclaw, WA 98022. The views expressed or implied in this work do not necessarily reflect those of Pleasant Word. The author(s) is ultimately responsible for the design, content and editorial accuracy of this work.

ISBN 1–4141–0033–7
Library of Congress Catalog Card Number: 2003111374

"When you pass through the waters, I will be with you; and when you pass through the rivers, they will not sweep over you. When you walk through the fire, you will not be burned; the flames will not set you ablaze" (Isaiah 43:2).

Table of Contents

Foreword 9
Acknowledgments 11
A Letter to the Reader 13

Life's Clock is Reset   Day 1 15
Stop the Trembling   Day 2 19
20–20 Vision   Day 3 23
Shout to the Lord   Day 4 27
The New Has Come   Day 5 31
How's Your Appetite?   Day 6 35
A Day of Hope   Day 7 39
Reflect on Your Reflection   Day 8 43
One Step at a Time   Day 9 47
Listen and Learn   Day 10 51
Isolation with God   Day 11 55
Alive in Christ   Day 12 59
No Place Like Home   Day 13 63
Why Me?   Day 14 67
Reach for the Mark   Day 15 71
Feast or Famine   Day 16 79

Is Your Cup Overflowing?   Day 17 83
Unmask the Fear   Day 18 87
Let's Make a Deal   Day 19 91
Nothing to Hide   Day 20 95
With a Rebel Yell . . .   Day 21 99
Yield to God   Day 22 103
Divine Appointment   Day 23 107
Let Go and Let God   Day 24 111
Something Better   Day 25 115
Valley of Despair   Day 26 119
Enough is Enough   Day 27 123
Let the Children Come   Day 28 127
His Image   Day 29 131
Refreshed Hearts   Day 30 135
From a Man's Perspective   Day 31 139

Index 145

Foreword

"Why do bad things happen to good people?"

It's an age–old question. Job didn't understand it, and neither did his so–called friends. The Apostle Paul didn't understand it, and so he pleaded with God three times to take away the thorn in his flesh that plagued him so. My husband, Dan, didn't understand it when his first wife died of cancer leaving him with 12–year–old twins to raise alone. I certainly didn't understand it when my first husband's insidious disease robbed him bit–by–bit first of his physical and mental health and finally, after ten years—right on the heels of a wildfire that destroyed our home and everything we owned—it took his life. And Wendi Calton didn't understand it when her trip home from high school camp that August day engulfed her in a horror that is seared into her forever.

"Why, God?" we demand. "Tell me why!"

But He doesn't explain.

What He does tell us is this: "My grace is sufficient for you, for my power is made perfect in weakness" (2 Corinthians 12:9).

Wendi's devotions are a perfect illustration of this scripture. They lead us on a blessed journey, away from self, away from fear and hopeless despair, and ever toward the heart of a loving God who is far bigger and greater than the circumstances of this suffering world.

Kay Marshall Strom
Author of "A Caregiver's Survival Guide" and other books

Acknowledgments

I owe much gratitude to my family who has encouraged me and supported me through the fires of life. Thank you for feeding me physically and spiritually.

Thank you for nurturing my wounded body and soul. Without each of you, I would not be who I am today. God has used you in a huge way to develop me as a person and as a child of God. You all are a gift given to me. What a joy it is to be a part of the family.

Finally, I would like to extend an extra special thanks to my husband Jim, for loving me as I am and for giving me four incredible boys. Josh, J.R., Jaeden, and Jacob, it is an honor to be your mom.

Wendi Sue

Dear reader,

I have the best news ever to share with you: the testimony of Jesus Christ and His love for you. Absolutely anyone can benefit from the love of God. This is my personal testimony of God's love for me. My prayer is that as you read this each day, you would know and experience the love of God, no matter where you have been or where you are headed.

If you are struggling with physical or emotional issues, my prayer is that you would overcome them with the power of God. Those of you who have been hospitalized; those of you stuck in an overwhelming situation; those who struggle with who God made you to be and His plan for you; those of you who are a parent or a grandparent and are in prayer for your children; and to those of you who can say "life is good" but need to be reminded that God truly is active today, I pray that this testimony will find you and that you will experience the peace of God.

> *1 John 5:9, 11–12*
>
> *"We accept man's testimony, but God's testimony is greater because it is the testimony of God, which he has given about his son" (verse 9).*
>
> *"And this is the testimony: God has given us eternal life, and this life is in his Son. He who has the Son has life; he who does not have the Son of God does not have life" (verses 11–12).*

Glory and honor to Him,
Wendi Sue Calton

All inquiries or comments regarding *Peace in a Flaming Storm* may be directed to Wendi Sue Calton (mailto:brandmarks4jc@hotmail.com). For the reader's information, all scripture quoted in this book is taken from the New International Version Study Bible.

Life's Clock is Reset

The snack shop was the final stop before the journey home. I bought a pack of gum. Sitting in the back seat popping bubbles, I never saw what was coming.

We came around a corner and a few people cried out. We hit something, another car I am told. But instead of stopping, it seemed as if we accelerated off the mountain, like a ball hit by a bat. The police report said we dropped two hundred feet off a cliff, below Highway 50 in the Lake Tahoe region of California.

I have no recollection of getting out of the van, no memory of the fire. Years later, I only know what I was told in the hospital. Apparently, I climbed out the back window of the crushed and burning van. I looked for a safe place to get away from the fire and to drop–and–roll, but I did not see one at first. Then I saw a small drop, ten feet or more, which was clear. That is where I jumped and began to roll out the flames.

What I remember to this day was the panic, trying to get up after the jump, but all I could do was lift my head. I can recall thinking,

"I have to get up! I have to get out of here." And then he was there. He was holding my hand, sharing my life and my pain. He lifted one of my hands up to show me the burns. Instead of one hand, I saw two hands; one was completely black and was raised up away from the other hand, which was blood red. He told me I had broken my back and help was on the way.

I thought the man was a doctor, the first to find me. I could hear voices so I knew people were looking for bodies. He asked me to sing with him. We sang "Jesus Loves Me." Instead of leaving me to get help, he brought Jesus to me. It was peace in a flaming storm. The panic went away, and the paramedics arrived.

> *The thief comes only to steal and kill and destroy; I have come that they may have life, and have it to the full (John 10:10).*

The paramedics told me that I was alone when they found me. They said there was no man with me, nobody was holding my hand or singing with me. I could tell them my phone number and everything that was happening; they said I was not in shock. Clearly, God had sent a guardian angel to protect me from the thief so that I may have life and have it to the full.

Two people died in that crash: Jimmie, who was sitting next to me on my left, and Donna, who was one seat over on my right. Many who knew them well told me that they had experienced Christ's love that week at Sierra Pines Baptist Camp. Jimmie and Donna knew the Savior and were prepared to go home.

My life–long battle began that day, Saturday, August 8, 1981, a soon–to–be freshman in high school. Life's clock had just been reset. But I had peace–I knew Jesus had come to give me life, life to the fullest. I knew Jesus would be there for this journey.

Whether your journey has just begun or you are in the thick of it, Jesus is there. He is there in the laughter, in the pain, the tears and the rejoicing. Can you recognize Him? Has your journey begun?

Take a moment and ask Him to reveal Himself to you, to meet you where you are today. Write down where you are in your journey. Pray for guidance and watch how the Lord travels along with you.

Thoughts & Prayers

_____
_____
_____
_____
_____
_____
_____
_____
_____
_____
_____
_____
_____
_____
_____
_____
_____
_____
_____
_____
_____
_____
_____

Stop the Trembling

I could see myself floating around the room, and sometimes I could see ants crawling all over me. The pain medicine was playing games with my mind. But no amount of medication could relieve the fact that I was always cold–extremely cold. My body trembled from the inside out, and I would beg for a warm blanket or for the heat lights to be turned on.

Despite my cold feeling, my body was actually burning with a temperature that was dangerously out of control. The staph infection I had contracted resulted in a fever so high, they were counting down the days of survival. The doctors and nurses were frantically trying to find a cure for the infection before my temperature hit that fatal level.

With each remedy of medicine they made up, they always had a scare to go with it, not knowing what side effects the new medicine might create. However, they explained to my parents, if they did not try new remedies, they would never cure the infection and would lose the battle for survival. Loss of eyesight, hearing, and even fertility problems were all on the list of side effects, but it was always worth the gamble.

As they struggled to find the right remedy, they also tried to find a way to calm me. They had no choice but to lay an ice blanket over me. I would cry and beg until I fell asleep. Yet over and over, my parents would say, "Pretend you are in the sun; think of warm things." They even put a poster of the beach on the wall for a visual. But the cold was too deep within. My mind could not begin to capture that feeling of warmth.

> *Finally, brothers, whatever is true, whatever is noble, whatever is right, whatever is pure, whatever is lovely, whatever is admirable– if anything is excellent or praiseworthy–think about such things. Whatever you have learned or received or heard from me, or seen in me–put it into practice. And the God of peace will be with you (Philippians 4:8–9).*

Have you ever had one of those days where you were out of control? There is just no peace and you cannot function. That is right where I was until the right medicine came along.

Stop the trembling–the right remedy, the cure for you is in the peace of God. Call upon His peace today.

Thoughts & Prayers

_____

_____

_____

_____

_____

_____

_____

_____

_____

_____

_____

_____

_____

_____

_____

_____

_____

_____

_____

_____

_____

_____

_____

_____

_____

_____

_____

Day 3

20–20 Vision

Abrush was part of my junior high school fashion statement. I carried it everywhere, constantly brushing my hair to keep that perfectly feathered look. No tweaks or flyaway hairs allowed. Every hair had to be in place.

This presented a huge problem when the nurses told me they had to shave my head. They could not risk infection. The hair had to go. Margo, my nurse, always got the worst job, and this time it was shaving my head.

She cinched up the striker frame and turned me to my stomach. I could not use my hands to stop the process but boy did my mouth put up a fight. I hollered, I cried, and I threatened to bite off her nose if she dared bend close enough. But she knew what needed to be done, and she began working through her task.

She snipped back my hair until it was short enough to use a disposable razor. I would feel the sharp sting of scabs being pulled off and then I would insult Margo for doing her job. It was a grueling task for her I am sure. To inflict pain in order to bring healing has to go against nature. In fact, other nurses made sure I knew I had made her cry and how rotten that was of me.

I could not see the big picture. I only thought of not having hair for the moment. Margo thought of my having hair to brush for a lifetime. She did what was necessary for me to have life, not for her to have good feelings.

> *Consider it pure joy, my brothers, whenever you face trials of many kinds, because you know that the testing of your faith develops perseverance. Perseverance must finish its work so that you may be mature and complete, not lacking anything (James 1:2–4).*

Our circumstance and our pain can blur our vision. We see a very limited, one–sided view. But to persevere and finish brings a complete product, mature, and lacking nothing. See the big picture and find joy in it.

Thoughts & Prayers

Day 4

. . . .

Shout to the Lord

B oy, did I have the best set of lungs in that hospital. For three months, anyone who visited or stayed there knew of the fourteen–year–old girl who had been burned. Three times a day I would get dressing changes where nurses would remove my bandages.

Do you hate the feeling of peeling off a band–aid? Try doing this with no skin. The process was horrific. The bandages were soaked with blood and pus. In fact, my arms were so swollen one time that the doctors had to run a razor blade down them just so they could release the extra fluid.

Yep, I screamed and cried with all I had. I did not swear, but every-one knew I was in pain. After the dressing change was completed, I would apologize over and over for yelling. "Please" and "thank you" were common words at that time as well. But several hours later, when they came to change my dressings yet again, I would proceed to shout at the top of my lungs until they were finished. I just wanted it to be over.

27

When I stop and listen, I do not hear it. In God's word, I do not hear the hollering and fighting of the pain Jesus endured for you and me. Listen to Mark's words in chapter 15, as he describes how Jesus handled the pain.

> *Wanting to satisfy the crowd, Pilate released Barabbas to them. He had Jesus flogged, and handed him over to be crucified. The soldiers led Jesus away into the palace and called together the whole company of soldiers. They put a purple robe on him, then twisted together a crown of thorns and set it on him. And they began to call out to him, "Hail, King of the Jews!" Again and again they struck him on the head with a staff and spit on him. Falling on their knees, they paid homage to him. And when they had mocked him, they took off the purple robe and put his own clothes on him. Then they led him out to crucify him (Mark 15:15–20).*

I did not hear it. No crying out and no fighting back. Jesus just took it for you and for me, and He took it from a whole company of soldiers. And the worst of it was this was not even the worst of it. The crucifixion was still to come. Soon He would endure the ultimate pain on the cross. The whipping was only the preliminary pain.

Is it not amazing how deep His love is for us? Praise Jesus for His enduring love.

Thoughts & Prayers

Day 5

• •

The New Has Come

The process of receiving new skin is no easy task. In fact, it gave me an ulcer. I knew pain and knew the process included a whole lot of it. The old skin needed to be peeled off (debried was the term the doctors used) and the limb needed to be scrubbed with Betadine (an orange anti-bacterial soap that stays around for weeks).

During the skin graft surgery, the doctors would peel good skin from a place on my body that had not been burned–similar to using a hot cheese slicer. Thin pieces of skin were sliced and placed on the limb that needed new skin. To hold the new skin in place, bridal veil (a fabric used in burn centers) was wrapped around and stapled to the limb. Stitches were too time consuming and most surgeons are not seamstresses. So, staples did the job.

Once the surgery was complete, time was to be the healer, along with the light and fresh air. Exposure was good. After a few weeks, it would be time to remove the bridal veil. The only problem was that the new skin was like one big scab that had grown around the veil. So the process was ugly.

31

To remove the bridal veil fabric, the doctors had to pluck each staple out and then they could begin pulling the veil (and the scabbing) off. Once it was all off, they brought in a large ultra violet light to dry out the open sores. The exposure to the "light" had great healing powers. Sure the new skin was scarred and not very attractive, but it was skin and it was a new creation.

> *Therefore, if anyone is in Christ, he is a new creation; the old has gone, the new has come! All this is from God, who reconciled us to himself through Christ (2 Corinthians 5:17–18a).*

How wonderful it is to know you are made new, to know the skin graft has taken, and the light is bringing more healing. It brings hope for the future. Just as when Christ receives us into His kingdom, we are grafted into His family and receive His healing powers.

To be a new creation in Christ is not always an easy task. Sometimes pain and suffering are involved. But, the "new has come!" Rejoice that He has brought you through the fire and has reconciled you in Christ–a new creation.

Recognize your fire. Write it down. Realize the Lord has healing power; praise Him for it. Rejoice, for you are being made new.

Thoughts & Prayers

_____

_____

_____

_____

_____

_____

_____

_____

_____

_____

_____

_____

_____

_____

_____

_____

_____

_____

_____

_____

_____

_____

_____

_____

_____

_____

_____

_____

_____

_____

Day 6

How's Your Appetite?

The feeding tube was by far the grossest thing. It enters through the nose and slides right down into the stomach. I gag just remembering the process of putting it in and taking it out. Sometimes it would clog or kink, and other times, I just needed a clean tube. It was just a sick process, but I could not digest solid foods for months and that tube gave me the protein I needed.

My meals always came in a special brown bag. The brown bag had been refrigerated so when the liquid contents went down my feeding tube, it was a cool feeling that seemed to coat my stomach. Like the Pepto-Bismol commercial that shows the pink coating flowing through the system–that is how it felt.

My sister occupied the bed next to mine. She too had severe burns from the same accident, but she escaped the feeding tube. Milk shakes, chocolate pies, pizzas, Captain La Comida tostadas, and on and on went the list of great foods she could eat. For a teenager, those were great foods.

That chocolate pie must have been four or five inches tall, packed high with cream. "If she will not eat it, bring it over here," I would say. But the same old words, "Sorry honey," would always come from the nurse's mouth. Then I would give my sister an earful for turning it away. "You could have at least taken a bite and told me if it was any good." Being the older sister, she would just ignore me and I would continue to hunger for the taste of real food.

Do you have a hunger for God's Word? I wish I hungered fervently for His Word like I did for that chocolate pie. I believe the people of Matthew 15 had that fervent hunger.

> *Jesus called his disciples to him and said, "I have compassion for these people; they have already been with me three days and have nothing to eat. I do not want to send them away hungry, or they may collapse on the way" (Matthew 15:32).*

I imagine some came to Jesus with a lunch and others with nothing. The more they heard Him speak, the more intense their hunger for Him became. Food was secondary; His words were a necessity for life. Do not go hungry; feast like the four thousand feasted–on His Word.

Thoughts & Prayers

_____

_____

_____

_____

_____

_____

_____

_____

_____

_____

_____

_____

_____

_____

_____

_____

_____

_____

_____

_____

_____

_____

_____

_____

_____

_____

_____

_____

_____

A Day of Hope

Isn't it great to run barefoot in the damp green grass, or wiggle your toes in a stream of cool water? Isn't it wonderful to take a full, deep breath of mountain–fresh air, especially after the rain? To walk, run or even wiggle my toes in a small stream of cool water seemed like a fantasyland. No one was entertaining those thoughts but me. Oh, how I wanted to walk again!

After breaking my back at vertebras T–11 and 12, there was little hope of ever being able to do any of these things. The doctors, unfortunately, could not surgically repair my back because of the state of the burns on the rest of my body. Also, by that time, I had caught staph infection, a very dangerous illness. There was too much risk of putting a patient in my condition under anesthesia for such a major surgery.

For sixteen weeks, I laid on a striker bed. It was like a Ferris wheel ride, only without the smiles and laughter. The striker bed was a large frame that rotated the bed end over end. I would lie on a mattress while the nurses placed a second mattress on top of me. They strapped a seatbelt around the two mattresses creating a tight sandwich. When all was secure, they would rotate the bed. One minute I was lying on my back, the next I had rotated up to a standing position. Then I would continue right on over to where I was lying on my stomach.

It was actually not that bad once I was on my stomach. There was a nice cut out for my face, similar to a massage table. And, I needed a different view every so often. I was stuck in that bed forever–or so it seemed.

I often dreamed of being on the other side of the door–the door that led to the nurses' station. I could hear laughter throughout the day, and it was always just on the other side of my door. It was my hope and dream that one day I would walk through that door and laugh along with the nurses.

I can remember the physical therapist coming to my room one day and plastering my body for a brace. He wrapped me in plastic wrap and molded my body with cool plaster. "This may work," the therapist said. I might be walking again soon, I thought. This was a day of hope, a breath of fresh air, perhaps a turning point.

> *He gives strength to the weary and increases the power of the weak.*
> *Even youths grow tired and weary and young men stumble and fall;*
> *but those who hope in the Lord will renew their strength. They will*
> *soar on wings like eagles; they will run and not grow weary, they*
> *will walk and not be faint (Isaiah 40:29–31).*

Walk in that green grass, wiggle your toes in streams of cool water, and breathe deeply that mountain fresh air. Hope in the Lord and He will renew your strength.

Thoughts & Prayers

_____

_____

_____

_____

_____

_____

_____

_____

_____

_____

_____

_____

_____

_____

_____

_____

_____

_____

_____

_____

_____

_____

_____

_____

_____

_____

_____

_____

_____

_____

_____

Day 8

Reflect on Your Reflection

I actually liked lying on my stomach as it gave me a different view; a view of lovely floor tiles. However, there was another plus to this position–a small stool could be placed on the floor under my face. On this stool, nurses would place letters that were written to me. I always enjoyed reading a special note from a friend. Another tool the nurses used was a double mirror. This set–up would keep me entertained for hours. One mirror caught the reflection of the television and the other mirror caught the first mirror's reflection. With the right angles, I could be happy as a clam, strapped upside down to a bed, watching my favorite television shows. Truth be told, this is where I was first introduced to soap operas (which was a hard habit to break). Regardless, the double mirror kept my mind off my situation.

What was my situation? I knew I had been burned. I felt the pain. But I honestly did not know the reality of it. After all, I had been told that everything was going to be great and things were looking good. "Great" and "good"–that sounded like there was really no problem.

Then one day those double mirrors painted a different picture–a reflection of reality. The nurse was adjusting the mirrors to catch the television's reflection but inadvertently caught the wrong reflection. For the first time since before the accident, I saw my face– swollen, blistered, red and purple, raw with several scabs. Reality was not "great" or even "good." I lost it. I threw up. I tossed the big cookie! I sobbed out of control.

Reality is not always a pretty picture. I relate it to Christ and think He did not like His picture of dying on the cross.

> *Jesus went out as usual to the Mount of Olives, and his disciples followed him. On reaching the place, he said to them, "Pray that you will not fall into temptation." He withdrew about a stone's throw beyond them, knelt down and prayed, "Father, if you are willing, take this cup from me; yet not my will, but yours be done." An angel from heaven appeared to him and strengthened him. And being in anguish, he prayed more earnestly, and his sweat was like drops of blood falling to the ground (Luke 22:39–44).*

Reality for Him brought sweat and blood. Yet He still looked out for His disciples, "Pray that you will not fall into temptation." He also looked to the will of the Father and not His own. And when His eyes were on the Father, "an angel appeared from heaven to Him and strengthened Him."

Reality is what it is, but fixing your eyes on the Father sure does change the picture. In fact, reflecting on the Father will improve your own reflection. Christ was strengthened and overcame death. What an awesome picture of sacrificial love.

Reality does not have to be ugly. Allow the Father to strengthen you and make an awesome picture. In your anguish, pray earnestly to the One who will give you strength. What is in your reflection today that needs to be given to the Lord?

Thoughts & Prayers

_____
_____
_____
_____
_____
_____
_____
_____
_____
_____
_____
_____
_____
_____
_____
_____
_____
_____
_____
_____
_____
_____
_____
_____
_____
_____
_____
_____

Day 9

One Step at a Time

Once the therapists had my back brace fitting like a glove, they took a few days to prepare my body for the shock of bearing weight. They would rotate my bed to a ninety–degree angle so that I was "standing" straight up. This would allow the blood to flow down through my legs.

Since my legs were not burned, the surgeons were able to use this part of my body for skin grafts to help other areas without skin. After removing the skin, my legs were treated just as if they had been burned and were then bandaged tightly. So when the striker bed was rotated straight up, I could feel the beads of blood popping through the newly forming skin on each leg. Later it began itching–a feeling that just seemed out of control. If you have ever had a cast and could not get under it to get the dry skin itch, you know the feeling.

I could only "stand" a few minutes the first few times before I had to lie down again. Despite the shortness of this "standing" feeling, I gained hope. In fact, the best thing about "standing" was that I saw the doorway of my hospital room. That first time, I set a goal

47

to walk straight out that door, one step at a time. And I was just going to keep on walking, step by step with Jesus.

> *To this you were called, because Christ suffered for you, leaving you an example, that you should follow in his steps. He committed no sin, and no deceit was found in his mouth. When they hurled their insults at him, he did not retaliate; when he suffered, he made no threats. Instead, he entrusted himself to him who judges justly. He himself bore our sins in his body on the tree, so that we might die to sins and live for righteousness; by his wounds you have been healed. For you were like sheep going astray, but now you have returned to the shepherd and overseer of your souls (1 Peter 2:21–25).*

What door do you need to walk through today? Follow Christ's example. Walk step by step with Jesus, trusting the One who judges justly. Find your door and take a step today.

Thoughts & Prayers

_____

_____

_____

_____

_____

_____

_____

_____

_____

_____

_____

_____

_____

_____

_____

_____

_____

_____

_____

_____

_____

_____

_____

_____

_____

_____

_____

• •

Listen and Learn

When the physical therapists first came to my hospital room, I enjoyed meeting new faces. They were handsome men who told me what I wanted to hear. "Everything will be fine. We will fix this. This will look great after we are done with it." And so I was excited about what they had to offer. They measured me for the Jobst suits, worked on a back brace, wiggled my fingers and toes, and made me laugh.

But things became painful. The wiggles turned into pulling, poking, and prodding. It got so bad that when I saw the physical therapists coming to my room, I would say, "Mom, lock the door. Do not let them in." Then she would just sort of laugh, give me that "I am sorry but you have to" look and leave the room. I would then have one of those moments when I would let everyone in the hospital know, through the piercing strength of my vocal cords, that the little burned girl was still alive. I screamed so much that those poor men became very frustrated and downhearted.

Although they spent several weeks trying to improve the flexibility in my joints, the physical therapists were getting nowhere. I refused to listen and I refused to follow directions. So they got serious. It was time to knock me out–put me under–just so they could bend my elbows, lift my arms and curl my fingers.

An anesthesiologist came to my room because this was considered a surgical procedure. After the first time of knocking me out and bending and twisting my stiff joints, it was a success. So they used this method of therapy for my body several more times.

How frustrating it must have been for these men, to know that there is such an easy solution. Move those joints and things will improve. Yet, I did not cooperate. In fact, I think I made myself even more miserable. After each therapy treatment, my body would be sore, and I had to deal with the aftereffects of the anesthesia.

> *Do not merely listen to the word, and so deceive yourselves. Do what it says. Anyone who listens to the word but does not do what it says is like a man who looks at his face in a mirror and, after looking at himself, goes away and immediately forgets what he looks like. But the man who looks intently into the perfect law that gives freedom, and continues to do this, not forgetting what he has heard, but doing it–he will be blessed in what he does (James 1:22–25).*

I bet God sometimes looks at us and says, "There is such an easy solution. Why do you not just stop your hollering and listen?"

If you can avoid the aftereffects of surgery, then do it! Stop–look–listen and do what God asks of you. There are freedom and blessings in Him.

Thoughts & Prayers

Day 11

....

Isolation with God

I t looked like a space capsule. The tube itself was glass, and the doors were large plates of steel. I would lie on a gurney bed, and the attendants would slide me into the tube. Once inside, they shut the door and sealed it tightly. You would think I was going to the moon.

The only person allowed in the room was the "healing tank" operator. His job was to make sure we did not ignite. You see, this tank was filled with 100% oxygen and was used to speed up the healing process for burns. The only problem was that it was risky business and complete isolation was required.

Before I could enter the "healing tank," I had to be stripped of everything. Every bandage and article of clothing had to be removed. Even the oil on my skin had to be cleaned. All of these items could potentially set off a spark and ignite the oxygen–filled tank. I was also told not to wiggle my toes as the nails could cause unwanted friction. I could not even grind my teeth. I was forced to relax every muscle.

Relax every muscle? That is a little difficult for a teenager who had been burned a few weeks before. Now I was being told to stay still to avoid blowing up inside this metal tank. I entered the tank completely vulnerable, with one white sheet draped over me. I was completely isolated from everyone and everything.

The "healing tank" operator was very friendly and worked on calming my fears by talking to me. As the oxygen entered the tank, I felt like I was going under water. The operator would tell me when my ears would begin popping and when deep breaths would be difficult. He watched the panel of gauges constantly and when we arrived at 100% oxygen, he would act like an airplane pilot. "To those passengers traveling in first class, welcome aboard. We have reached our cruising altitude of 100% oxygen. Lie back and enjoy our feature presentation. We will arrive back at Chico Hospital in approximately one hour. Thank you for choosing the oxygen tank."

Each time I went to the tank, it became a little easier and less stressful. I could actually relax and watch a television program through the glass panels in the tube.

For maximum healing, I had to be completely isolated from my world and placed in a tank with a proven healer–oxygen. Today, I have to do that very same thing–isolate myself with the proven Healer. I have to come into the presence of God, just Him and me. Here there is peace. I can relax, and the healing can begin.

Jesus sets a fantastic example for us to follow.

> *Very early in the morning, while it was still dark, Jesus got up, left the house and went off to a solitary place, where he prayed. Simon and his companions went to look for him, and when they found him, they exclaimed: "Everyone is looking for you!" (Mark 1:35–37).*

Throughout the gospels, you learn that this is a pattern of Christ. In Matthew 6:5, Jesus tells us how to be in prayer, alone with God. Matthew 14:23 shows us how Jesus went to the mountain top to pray by Himself. And Matthew 26:36 explains how Jesus told His disciples to sit while He went away to pray.

Each book of the gospels, Matthew, Mark, Luke, and John, record Jesus taking time to be alone with God in prayer. It was vital for Christ to do this in order for Him to keep His focus on His calling. God called Him to be an example for us, and He called Him to be the ultimate sacrifice so that we may know the love of God.

God has called you to be an example as well, to share the love of God. How are you to know what to share with others if you have not had your own isolated focus time? Perhaps God wants you to be a messenger for another person. You may not ever deliver that message if you have not first received it from Him. His word is for you and for those you can reach.

Today, isolate yourself with God. Ask Him to give you an applicable message in His Word that you can share with a friend this week. Write down that message and let God use you as His divine messenger.

Thoughts & Prayers

_____

_____

_____

_____

_____

_____

_____

_____

_____

_____

_____

_____

_____

_____

_____

_____

_____

_____

_____

_____

_____

_____

_____

_____

_____

_____

_____

_____

Alive in Christma

I can remember this as if it was yesterday. I had just learned to walk again, and my sister had made me potato and onion soup. I needed to gain weight, so my mother asked me to walk to the cafeteria to warm the soup. I was nervous about seeing people; I knew I was a sad sight: five foot, three inches tall, weighing only seventy–five pounds, wearing a back brace, an elastic compression suit (Jobst suit in medical terms) that covered me from head to toe, and a bright, royal–purple bathrobe.

To get the full picture, imagine a thick nylon stocking pulled over your head that has a circle cut out for the face plus two holes for the ears. The little hair you have is sticking out the ear holes, and you are very pale because you have not been outside for nearly three months.

So I chose to lean against the wall by the cafeteria door while my mom used the microwave to warm the soup. I guess I had no idea how bad I really looked. A hospital volunteer walked out of the cafeteria door and hung a sharp left directly into me. She let out a loud holler as her words stabbed me like a knife, "It's alive."

Today, I can look back and laugh because I *am* alive–alive in Christ. He who is rich in mercy, made me alive even when I was dead (and looking it too). By His grace, I have been made alive with His spirit living and breathing in me.

> *But because of his great love for us, God, who is rich in mercy, made us alive with Christ even when we were dead in transgressions–it is by grace you have been saved (Ephesians 2:4–5).*

I challenge you today. Take a good look inside yourself. Are you living and breathing God's Word or are you among the walking dead? Grab hold, experience His mercy and grace and live a full life "alive in Christ!"

Thoughts & Prayers

Day 13

. . . .

No Place Like Home

My first visit home was on October 31. I was out of the hospital on a day pass, and I could not wait to go to the town Halloween Festival. It was to be held at the elementary school, and all my friends were awaiting my arrival. They expected me to walk in looking the way they had known me–friendly, outgoing, and the life of the party.

I walked up to one of my friends named Brian. "Hi Brian," I said. "What are you supposed to be?" Brian asked. "Nothing," I said. And then I walked away.

Inside, I was crushed. Did I really look that bad, like I was in some kind of freaky Halloween costume? My expectations of returning home were shot. Three months had gone by and life had moved on, and so had some friends.

But I was finally walking, and my body was working overtime to continue the healing process. I was out of the hospital, breathing fresh air. I needed to have some fun to be refreshed and renewed in life.

63

Soon word got out that I had arrived at the Halloween Festival, and several friends came to my side. It was hard to be around so many eyes that just could not stop staring at me. I suggested we go trick–or–treating and take advantage of my unique costume. The cool air was soothing, and I finally began to relax.

The "life of the party" in me began to show itself. I suggested we head for the town cemetery. Besides, how much trouble could a group of freshmen kids cause on Halloween in a cemetery anyway? It truly was a hoot of a good time. I would stand behind a tombstone and hide until little kids came walking by. When the trick–or–treaters innocently came near me, my friends would begin to make their freaky noises and would send me walking out towards the kids. The kids would scream and run. Some even dropped their bags of candy and we grabbed them, laughing hysterically.

> *Therefore we do not lose heart. Though outwardly we are wasting away, yet inwardly we are being renewed day by day. For our light and momentary troubles are achieving for us an eternal glory that far outweighs them all. So we fix our eyes not on what is seen, but on what is unseen. For what is seen is temporary, but what is unseen is eternal (2 Corinthians 4:16–18).*

Our circumstance can definitely affect our emotions and ultimately ruin our day. But it does not have to. Fix your eyes on the unseen– His eternal glory–and be refreshed and renewed day by day.

Thoughts & Prayers

_____

_____

_____

_____

_____

_____

_____

_____

_____

_____

_____

_____

_____

_____

_____

_____

_____

_____

_____

_____

_____

_____

_____

_____

_____

_____

_____

. . . .

Why Me?

Poor Charlie Brown, things have gone wrong again. His kite is in a tree; he is tangled up in the kite and hanging by his ankles. Charlie says, "Why me?" I remember that poster hanging in my room. I do not know if I bought it, but I know I bought the attitude for quite a while.

I did not see how this was going to work out. I could not even get out of bed in the morning without my mother's help. My body hurt to walk. To move my arms and have the open sores rub together in the pit of my arms was extremely uncomfortable. We put small sponges under my arms for a little relief. My neck and shoulders felt stuck in place with very little or no motion to them. I was a walking broomstick (skinny, bald, and brown in a Jobst suit).

How long was I going to be like this? I was told I would play basketball, run with my friends, cheerlead, or whatever I wanted. And yet I was stuck in a body that could hardly move. My skin had very little elasticity. I really was stuck in a body I did not want. "Why me?"

I had a lot of time to ponder Charlie's and my situation. Three years in that Jobst suit, and there was no easy answer. I am just thankful that God is God, and I am not. I have learned that it is not about my pity party or me. It is about God doing a good work in me and my being in partnership with Him. Then the good work He is doing in me can be brought to completion. Plus, it can be passed on to you and others.

> In all my prayers for all of you, I always pray with joy because of your partnership in the gospel from the first day until now, being confident of this, that he who began a good work in you will carry it on to completion until the day of Christ Jesus (Philippians 1:4–6).

Just as Paul prayed for the Philippians that God's good work would be carried out to completion, I pray this prayer for you as well. For twenty–one years later, I am playing basketball with my four sons, I ran a marathon with friends, and now I am sharing with you.

The day of completion in Christ has yet to come–but I can see beyond the hurt, the scars, the looks and comments of people and say God is doing a good work. Praise God!

Thoughts & Prayers

_____
_____
_____
_____
_____
_____
_____
_____
_____
_____
_____
_____
_____
_____
_____
_____
_____
_____
_____
_____
_____
_____
_____
_____
_____
_____
_____
_____

❀ ❀

Reach for the Mark

I must admit my mother and I had a love/hate relationship going on for a few years–but only because she loved me enough to do what was good–no, best–for me. I always say, "If I can become half the woman that my mom is, I know I will have accomplished something in my lifetime." God gave her an abundance of courage during my healing years.

My mother was determined not to have a cripple for a daughter because she knew it did not have to be that way. I can remember struggling with the area directly behind my armpits. The scar tissue was growing a web and severely limiting my range of motion. To lift my arm to shoulder level was a struggle.

My mom agreed with the physical therapist that it would be best to go in for (yet another) surgery and have those webs snipped out. I was not happy. I hated surgery, but I did it–and I expressed my anger the entire way. After it was over, I was relieved but only until I figured out that they made an airplane splint for my right arm during the process.

I had to be a humorous sight to see. I was probably just plain pathetic–skinny as a rail, covered from head to toe in the nylon Jobst suit, ski cap on my bald head, body brace, and now an airplane splint that held my arm straight out for weeks. I know I tried to give my mom a Samurai chop a few times with that thing. But that did not stop her.

Once that splint came off, she began marking on the wall how high I could raise my arm. Each time I had to raise it higher than the time before, or she would do it for me. I used to put my arm on the kitchen table and slowly kneel down until I felt the tissue on my arm give way. Neither my mom nor I wanted to go back for more surgery and certainly not another round with that airplane splint. I believe the physical therapist even threatened me with a permanent cast if I did not work at it.

> *Therefore, prepare your minds for action; be self–controlled; set your hope fully on the grace to be given you when Jesus Christ is revealed. As obedient children, do not conform to the evil desires you had when you lived in ignorance. But just as he who called you is holy, so be holy in all you do; for it is written: "Be holy, because I am holy" (1 Peter 1:13–16).*

My mother gave me a vision–to reach that mark every day and then to reach a little higher. What mark is it that God is calling you to reach? Is He calling you to be holy in your values, in your marriage, or with your friendships?

Or perhaps there are other areas in your life where God has identified a vision to achieve. Set a goal to identify this mark and then go for it! Be what you have been called to be–"you are not a cripple." Reach the highest mark.

Thoughts & Prayers

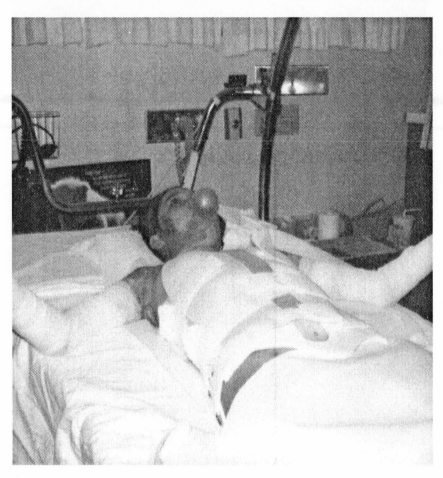

My enthusiasm was high, as I had been fitted for a body brace that would support my broken back and potentially allow me to walk again.

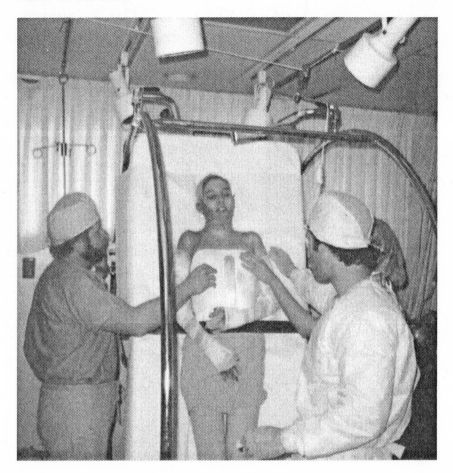

When preparing to walk, the striker frame bed helped to balance my frail body. Photo taken in October of 1981, two and a half months after the accident.

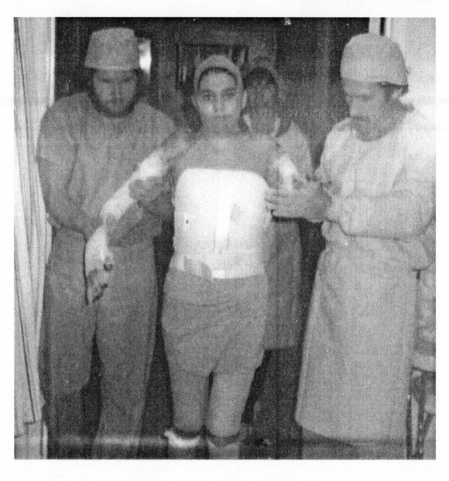

Once out of bed, I just wanted to keep on walking right out of that hospital.

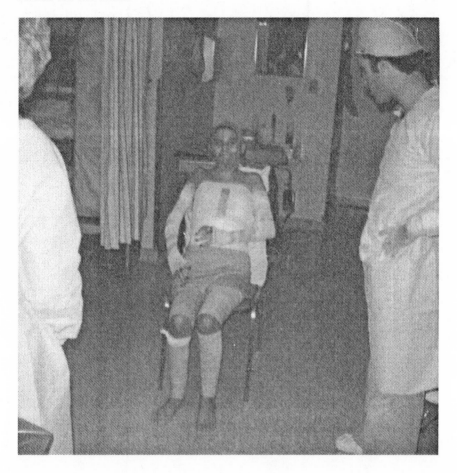

Sitting was a huge accomplishment after lying down for almost three months.

Even though the scars remain on the outside, inside there has been tremendous healing. Today, I find great joy in my family and the blessings of being alive continue to overflow.

Feast or Famine

Somehow, I had exhausted all of my resources. No one felt sorry for me any more. I must have been completely ungrateful. So there I sat, looking at my grilled cheese sandwich and no one would feed me.

I did not like to bend my elbows. My skin would not stretch; it was uncomfortable and just felt like it would rip. I could not get my skin to cooperate. It was frustrating for me and, in return, I frustrated others.

So I sat, like a puppy dog begging for food. I just stared at that sandwich wishing it would somehow magically make its way into my mouth. After lots of wishful thinking, I finally took action. I went to the kitchen drawer and took out a long wooden spoon and a fork. I got some tape and attached that fork, and an angle, onto the end of the wooden spoon so that when I held the spoon, even if I could not bend my elbow, the fork would head right toward my mouth.

Now I had something to work with. I stabbed that sandwich, bent my elbow about two inches and stretched my neck out as far as I could. I finally was able to feed myself, one bite at a time. I did it! It took a long time when I tried to eat, as I could not stand to keep my elbow bent for very long.

Each meal after that, I became more and more creative. I taped forks and spoons on the long wooden spoon several times. Meal times became therapy sessions and, little by little, my elbows began to give and my skin began to stretch. I was on my way to some real nourishment. I began craving all kinds of foods and enjoyed the challenge of being fed–by me.

> *Therefore, rid yourselves of all malice and all deceit, hypocrisy, envy, and slander of every kind. Like newborn babies, crave pure spiritual milk, so that by it you may grow up in your salvation, now that you have tasted that the Lord is good (1 Peter 2:1–3).*

Sometimes it is hard to see yourself and the attitude you have built up toward life until you have exhausted those around you. You begin to wonder how you got into this predicament. Then you take action. You feast on God's Word.

Do you need a feast today? Crave spiritual milk. Taste and know that the Lord is good. Feast on His Word.

Thoughts & Prayers

Day 17

Is Your Cup Overflowing?

There is little that is more frustrating than your mind telling your body to do something, and the body just cannot per-form.

From what I understand, if you do not use your joints, they can lock up. For instance, if the elbow is not "worked"–bent open and closed–then it can freeze and you will only have limited use of it in the future. Therefore, if I wanted my body to function normally, constant use and physical therapy was a must.

My physical therapist had all kinds of gizmos that gave my body a workout. For my hands, I needed to wear braces a few times a day. These braces were similar to an arm splint–plastic on the bottom of the forearm with a Velcro wrapping to hold it in place.

The hand and forearm rested on it like on the arm of a chair. It had rubber bands attached to the plastic, and the bands had Velcro straps attached to them. Each finger had its own band and strap so when it was attached, the finger would be pulled down and begin the process of making a fist. I wore the braces a few hours each day, and I saw it as one more thing that made me look abnormal.

My vision was limited. I could not see past the present. Holding a pencil or a can of Pepsi, taking change from the grocery clerk, tying my shoes, brushing my hair or teeth, driving a car–all of these and so many more, would not be possible unless I wore those braces daily. It was a necessity if I was to have a future.

If we are to have a future with God, should not being in His Word daily be a necessity? Your vision might be slightly blurred–perhaps you are pre–occupied half the time. But with God, you have a future. Turning the pages of the Bible is spiritual therapy.

> For just as the sufferings of Christ flow over into our lives, so also through Christ our comfort overflows. If we are distressed, it is for your comfort and salvation; if we are comforted, it is for your comfort, which produces in you patient endurance of the same sufferings we suffer (2 Corinthians 1:5–6).

Today I can turn my hands so the palms are facing up while placing them together so as to make a cup. For me, that is a huge accomplishment. But when I stop and look inside, my cup is not empty. Instead, my cup is filled with the presence and joy of the Lord.

Do not let your cup be empty today. Find comfort in His Word.

Thoughts & Prayers

_____
_____
_____
_____
_____
_____
_____
_____
_____
_____
_____
_____
_____
_____
_____
_____
_____
_____
_____
_____
_____
_____
_____
_____
_____
_____
_____
_____
_____

Unmask the Fear

After my run–in with the double mirror, the mirror was no longer my friend. I avoided it at all costs. There were times when my mom would have me face it, and she would brush out my hair. I hated the way the burns had caused the right side of my face to droop.

The scar tissue runs down my hairline, out two inches, down to my chin, then off to the right and down my neck. The scar was so tight it pulled my eye and mouth down. My smile was lopsided, and my eye was slanted. Turning my head to the left was not a good feeling and something I tried to avoid. My eye was pulled so thin it almost shut, and my mouth felt like it was being stretched to my ear. What was I going to do with this face?

My hair had grown out and my mom thought I should go for a Jobst suit (actually more of a mask in this case) that allowed my hair to show. I thought it was a great idea; time to let my hair down! But, of course, when we talked to the doctors about it, they had other ideas. Another surgery.

Of all the surgeries, this was the only one I was remotely happy about. It was meant to smooth out the scar tissue on my face and release the hold it had on my eye and mouth. If all went well, my smile would not droop nearly as much and my vision would not blur when I turned my head to the left. Then I could let my hair down with a Jobst suit that showed more of my face and my hair.

A few months later, I was wearing the latest fashion in burn wear, a stylish Jobst suit that wrapped around my neck, up over my chin, and stretched from one ear to the other. A thin strap on each side followed my hair line up to the part in my hair, then traveled up and over my head and connected to the back of my Jobst suit at the neck line. It was a new me. But eventually, I would have to be completely unmasked. That thought really caused anxiety and fear of the unknown.

> *Therefore I tell you, do not worry about your life, what you will eat or drink; or about your body, what you will wear. Is not life more important than food, and the body more important than clothes? Look at the birds of the air; they do not sow or reap or store away in barns, and yet your heavenly Father feeds them. Are you not much more valuable than they? Who of you by worrying can add a single hour to his life? (Matthew 6:25–27).*

We all have those areas in life that seem to have a hold on us. They stretch us and they make us feel a bit on the uncomfortable side. They blur our vision. We like to avoid them, but they are always there–hidden worries or fears. Unmask your fear before your heavenly Father. You are valuable. He will take care of you.

Thoughts & Prayers

_____
_____
_____
_____
_____
_____
_____
_____
_____
_____
_____
_____
_____
_____
_____
_____
_____
_____
_____
_____
_____
_____
_____
_____
_____
_____
_____
_____

Day 19

Let's Make a Deal

It rained all day. The storm seemed to get worse as night fell. Inside, my soul was in turmoil. I found no joy in my circum stance. My dad said that it was time to get back into life and that meant back to school–high school. For the last six months, I was working with a home tutor trying to stay at class level.

How was I ever going to walk down a crowded hall, open a locker, hold a pencil, eat lunch, or use the washroom? To that day, I had not done any of those things by myself. I thought I might make a deal with the devil himself if I could just go back to being me, without the burns.

As I lay in bed listening to the thunder and the rain, I contemplated my situation and wondered if I could sell out my soul for a new life. I fell asleep, exhausted from the tears of emotions and ashamed of my ridiculous thoughts.

The worst of the storm had to be directly overhead. A loud crackle of thunder roared, and my eyes popped open. Looking to my window, I saw a figure cloaked with a cape. When lightening struck, I

91

saw the figure clearer. With all I had, I screamed at the top of my lungs, "DAD!" Every light in the house switched on. And when they did, reality became clear. There was my sister, standing by my window, wrapped in a blanket watching the storm.

I broke and let out my own storm of emotions as I explained how terrified I was that I might have actually sold out to the devil. How could I have even entertained those thoughts? I was fearful for my own salvation.

> *For you did not receive a spirit that makes you a slave again to fear, but you received the Spirit of sonship. And by him we cry, "Abba, Father." The Spirit himself testifies with our spirit that we are God's children. Now if we are children, then we are heirs— heirs of God and co–heirs with Christ, if indeed we share in his sufferings in order that we may also share in his glory (Romans 8:15–17).*

Have you been there—doubting whether or not you are a child of God? What a wonderful gift of peace to be assured you have the Father, the Son, and the Holy Spirit. Amen!

Thoughts & Prayers

Nothing to Hide

I had many fears about returning to school. The biggest had to be friends. Who would want to be my friend?

The bell rang; the hall began to fill with my high school peers. I thought I stuck out. Then I saw a familiar face–Sandy. She had always been good for a laugh and always wore a beautiful big smile. We ran track together just the year before. We were part of the relay team, and she was fast. In fact, she would always run the last leg of each race. She always challenged me to go the distance in everything.

"What's going on Caldie?" she yelled. (Caldie is my maiden name, and Sandy always called me by my last name.) I thought I would die–she was drawing attention to me. Not like I was not noticeable already. But come on; can we talk a little quieter? Then off it came. She pulled that ski cap right off that bald head of mine.

As I look back, I have no idea why I thought I looked better with that hat on–as if people would not know my head appeared bald with that Jobst suit on. But I tried to hide it anyway.

Sandy tossed my hat around, laughed, told a few bald jokes, and then went into the washroom with my hat. I was not going to follow her. I could push the door open, but once I was inside, I would be stuck. There was no way my arms would be able to pull that door open, nor would I be able to move fast enough to get through once it was open. So I waited, eyes shifting side to side to see how many kids noticed me.

One by one, they rubbed my bald head as they headed for class. Soon, Sandy came out of the bathroom, placed my cap back on my head, gave me a big hug, and said, "You're all right Caldie."

> For you created my inmost being; you knit me together in my mother's womb. I praise you because I am fearfully and wonderfully made; your works are wonderful, I know that full well. My frame was not hidden from you when I was made in the secret place. When I was woven together in the depths of the earth, your eyes saw my unformed body. All the days ordained for me were written in your book before one of them came to be (Psalms 139:13–16).

I do not know if she planned that little activity, but she taught me a huge lesson. You cannot hide who you are or who God has made you to be.

Your life has been planned, ordained, by God. There is nothing to hide. You are fearfully and wonderfully made. Be confident in Him, your Creator, today.

Thoughts & Prayers

_____

_____

_____

_____

_____

_____

_____

_____

_____

_____

_____

_____

_____

_____

_____

_____

_____

_____

_____

_____

_____

_____

_____

_____

_____

_____

_____

_____

With a Rebel Yell . . .

Why did I have to be the guinea pig for this new procedure? I had already had enough. Another surgery–cosmetic sur–gery–but who really cared? I was done. I just wanted to be a teenager. But my opinion did not seem to matter.

I went under the knife once again. During this surgery, the doctors cut along the edge of my burn and inserted a balloon underneath the neighboring good skin. The doctors would then complete the surgery by stapling my skin closed. This balloon–type device that was under my skin had a tail attached to it and at the end of the tail was a disk. The disk was used to receive injections of saline solu-tion that would then flow down the tail and into the balloon. As the balloon expanded with additional saline, my good skin would stretch. It was to be a six–week process.

Each day, I received an injection of the saline solution. My mom and a neighbor, who happened to be a registered nurse, gave me these daily injections. They would feel around the surface of the skin to find the disk, and then they would use a needle to inject additional solution. Each day these balloons would grow a little bigger, and the good skin would stretch a little more. Eventually, there would be enough extra good skin to be used to cover areas where there was no skin.

I had three of these balloons inserted into my body. One was located on each bicep and a third one above my right breast. By the time four weeks came around and all three balloons were inflated, I looked like a three–breasted Popeye. But I was still a teenager, and I just wanted to have fun.

At week five, I had to go to a Billy Idol concert, and there was no way around it. I had no idea what I was getting into. With all of those spiked collars and bracelets that people were wearing, I was afraid I was going to get popped. I tried to stay out of the crowds to avoid the spikes, and I was doing pretty well. But then the music started. The music was pumping through those speakers so loudly that it caused my saline filled balloons to vibrate. My enlarged arms and my inflated chest seemed to vibrate from the inside out. I had no idea how much damage the pounding music was causing to the healing process.

I popped staples, caused infections, and ended up back in surgery within a couple of days after the concert. Why did I have to be such a rebel? It was not worth it. It was stressful trying to keep my balloons away from those spikes. And it was painful enduring the infection that had set in. What was I thinking?

I imagine we all have asked that question a time or two. We all struggle with the sinful nature. Why do we do the things we do, or say the things we say? Even dear Paul struggled. Confusion set in as he struggled with his old self of sin and new self in Christ.

> I do not understand what I do. For what I want to do I do not do, but what I hate I do. And if I do what I do not want to do, I agree that the law is good. As it is, it is no longer I myself who do it, but it is sin living in me. I know that nothing good lives in me, that is,

in my sinful nature. For I have the desire to do what is good, but I cannot carry it out. For what I do is not the good I want to do; no, the evil I do not want to do–this I keep on doing. Now if I do what I do not want to do, it is no longer I who do it, but it is sin living in me that does it. So I find this law at work: When I want to do good, evil is right there with me. For in my inner being I delight in God's law; but I see another law at work in the members of my body, waging war against the law of my mind and making me a prisoner of the law of sin at work within my members. What a wretched man I am! Who will rescue me from this body of death? Thanks be to God–through Jesus Christ our Lord! So then, I myself in my mind am a slave to God's law, but in the sinful nature a slave to the law of sin (Romans 7:15–25).

I picture Paul sickened with himself, his actions, and his works–in anguish over sin. "What a sinful man I am!" I am sure he yelled those words, crying out to God, "Who will rescue me from this body of death?"

Reality can sure set in fast. We need rescuing! We need emergency surgery by God to repair the damage we have caused. "Thanks be to God–through Christ Jesus our Lord!"

Give thanks to Him for His victorious rescue.

Thoughts & Prayers

_____

_____

_____

_____

_____

_____

_____

_____

_____

_____

_____

_____

_____

_____

_____

_____

_____

_____

_____

_____

_____

_____

_____

_____

_____

_____

_____

_____

Yield to God

I would like to believe I was not alone and that every high school kid had some sort of identity crisis, big or small. Mine was prob ably on the large side. I was not feeling pretty and popular, smart and energetic, or even gifted and artsy. There was no boyfriend or even a best friend. No group was my group. For the first few years of high school, I just did not know how I fit in.

Then I got a car! I drove it off the lot with only three miles on it. A 1984 Honda Prelude, blue with pin stripes, a sunroof and all. My dad gave me a gas card and a checkbook. My monthly allowance was at least six times that of my other classmates.

This was the key that unlocked friendships. You buy them–you got them. From that point on, I was the designated driver. I got to go to every party, game, and social event. And, you guessed it, this spelled trouble.

Fast driving, alcohol, drugs, and a bad attitude were quickly intro-duced to me. The fast pace was my pace–until the emergency brake was pulled. I was accused of drug trafficking. Me? I could count on one hand how many times I had touched the stuff. But, I had touched the stuff. And, I had a car and had bought the wrong lifestyle.

I wanted to fit in so badly that I bought a lifestyle that could only lead to destruction. I honestly thought that people would see me as the fun girl, not the burned girl, if I went along with their craziness. Then I would have an identity and people would like me. I cared too much about what other people thought. My emphasis on life was all backwards, and it led to sin.

> *Let us throw off everything that hinders and the sin that so easily entangles, and let us run with perseverance the race marked out for us. Let us fix our eyes on Jesus, the author and perfecter of our faith, who for the joy set before him endured the cross, scorning its shame, and sat down at the right hand of the throne of God. Consider him who endured such opposition from sinful men, so that you will not grow weary and lose heart (Hebrews 12:1b–3).*

I thank the Lord that my emergency brake was pulled, that I was able to get out of that little car of mine and open my eyes to the sinful lifestyle I was in. Never again do I want to put others' opinions above God's. Christ did not do this, instead He fixed His eyes on God and He endured the humiliation as He was cursed, hit, and spit upon. He finished His race, and He was victorious.

Do you need to pull that emergency brake? Do you need to yield to God today? If so, do it. Be reminded of Christ's victory, be encouraged, do not grow weary and lose heart. Instead, praise Him for opening your eyes so that you may throw off everything that hinders and see the glorious finish with Him.

Write down what hinders you. Then, draw a line through it and release it to Him and claim victory in the name of Jesus.

Thoughts & Prayers

_____
_____
_____
_____
_____
_____
_____
_____
_____
_____
_____
_____
_____
_____
_____
_____
_____
_____
_____
_____
_____
_____
_____
_____
_____
_____
_____

Divine Appointment

When I graduated from high school, I had no clue what I was going to do. I got a job at Jack–in–the–Box, a fast food restaurant. But it was not going to last because I was only allowed to flip burgers in the back. It would not be appropriate to take money from customers and possibly interrupt their meal with the look of my hands. I was very discouraged with people and even with myself. This made me a prime candidate for my sister's suggestion.

"Let's go to camp," she stated. "The Christian camp we went to as kids needs counselors." I was in no shape to be a counselor for young girls. I had made a mess of my pre–teen and teenage years. But, I needed a change of scenery, so I went.

Week after week, I had a cabin full of eight girls. Two weeks were middle school students, one week junior high, and one week was spent with the high school work crew for family camp. Sharing my life with these girls softened my heart to God's calling for me. It not only softened me, but it changed my life and gave me direction.

One week, I had the most beautiful girls in my cabin. All the boy campers sought out their attention. But the attention of my girls was directed towards a good–looking male counselor. They spent all of their free time working to set me up. Every meal they sat next to his table, every group meeting they sat next to his cabin, and every game we played, we had to be teammates.

A definite attraction formed on my part, but to have a relationship with a young man like him seemed out of my league. I even said to a friend, "That is the kind of guy I would like to marry some day."

After camp was over, I was again asking those directional questions of, "What do I do now?" So I decided to go to Bible college–Christian Heritage College located in Southern California. Culture shock was what it was. But once again, my heart was transformed to seek out God–to know Him more.

That next summer, I went back to camp counseling and so did that good–looking young man. By the end of the summer, we had begun dating. Six years later, we were married. One of Jim's comments will always ring true in my ear. "I probably would not have looked twice at you before you were burned. I was never attracted to girls who thought so highly of themselves."

I do not have to guess–I know I was in the right place at the right time. Sometimes we look at an accident and say, "They were in the wrong place at the wrong time." Maybe not–perhaps we have a divine appointment, and we have been strategically placed for the glory of God.

Like David and Goliath, David was only a shepherd boy taking lunch to his brothers. From that, he not only killed Goliath, but also became king and a man after God's own heart. Like Esther, the Jewish queen of Persia, married to King Xerxes, she was placed in a position to save her people–the Jewish race. This she did and faced her divine appointment successfully. Like Jesus, in the Garden of Gethsemane–His accuser and betrayer Judas faced him. From there, His divine appointment was in full progress and would ultimately take place on the cross.

Divine appointments do not stop in God's Word. They continue in His people. I believe my van accident was hardly an accident. It was the beginning of my divine appointment with God. The people at Jack–in–the–Box may have thought someone could lose their appetite over my appearance but, on the other hand, my husband would not have looked twice if I had not been transformed. God planned my life, and I was strategically positioned.

Hear Mordecai's words to Esther.

> *He sent back this answer: "Do not think that because you are in the king's house you alone of all the Jews will escape. For if you remain silent at this time, relief and deliverance for the Jews will arise from another place, but you and your father's family will perish. And who knows but that you have come to royal position for such a time as this?" (Esther 4:13–14).*

We all have our time when God transforms us and places us in a strategic position to bring glory to Him. Reflect on your life. Write down a few of those times that God gave you a divine appointment. Give Him praise and ask to be used again and again.

Thoughts & Prayers

_____

_____

_____

_____

_____

_____

_____

_____

_____

_____

_____

_____

_____

_____

_____

_____

_____

_____

_____

_____

_____

_____

_____

_____

_____

_____

_____

_____

_____

Let Go and Let God

Four years to the day after my accident, August 8, 1985, I was invited to share my story with a youth group in Santa Clara, California. I attended their camp out and shared all the right words: Count it all joy, God not only saved me once but twice, His grace is sufficient for me; and on and on I went. But deep down, I was struggling with the direction my life had gone.

After the time of sharing at the campfire, the youth pastor singled me out and took me on a walk. He asked me a hard question, "Do you believe in what you said to those high school students? If you have issues with God, tell Him about it." That was the only invitation I needed.

I kicked at the dirt, picked up and threw rocks, and just laid into God. "I do not want to be a pawn in Your game! I am tired of this! When will this be over, this game of Yours?" I was throwing the best tantrum of my life. I dropped down in the dirt and just sobbed, "I am tired of fighting this."

Why I ever thought I could fight God's plan for me and win, I do not know. But I realized something very important that night. Yes, God did indeed save me twice: once from the fiery lake of eternity and once from the fiery blaze of the van. Yes, His grace is indeed sufficient. There is no other grace that makes me complete or that can allow me to see my trials as joy. Only through God can this be. So why not let go of my issues and simply let God do His thing, both in me and through me? Do not fight it, just give it over to Him. It was time to let go and let God.

> To keep me from becoming conceited because of these surpass-ingly great revelations, there was given me a thorn in my flesh, a messenger of Satan, to torment me. Three times I pleaded with the Lord to take it away from me. But he said to me, "My grace is sufficient for you, for my power is made perfect in weakness." Therefore I will boast all the more gladly about my weaknesses, so that Christ's power may rest on me. That is why, for Christ's sake, I delight in weaknesses, in insults, in hardships, in persecu-tions, in difficulties. For when I am weak, then I am strong (2 Corinthians 12:7–10).

Apostle Paul knew this well. He too wrestled with God. He saw his thorn as a daily reminder of Christ's power. I, too, have that daily reminder each time I look in the mirror. But today, I look back at what I see in the mirror and I smile. For, "when I am weak, then I am strong." Let go and let God.

Thoughts & Prayers

_____

_____

_____

_____

_____

_____

_____

_____

_____

_____

_____

_____

_____

_____

_____

_____

_____

_____

_____

_____

_____

_____

_____

_____

_____

_____

_____

Day 25

Something Better

As I got older and began to see Christians with different theological up–bringing, I faced a new challenge. Many times, I was asked if I had attended faith seminars. I even was told, "If you only had enough faith, God could remove those scars and make you new." That sounded good–remove my scars and make me new.

So I would lie in bed and claim I had faith that could move mountains. My eyes were squeezed shut and I would say, "I am willing if You are willing, Lord." Then I would open my eyes, look at my hands, and begin to cry.

I eventually went to a faith and healing seminar where God opened my eyes. I was eighteen years old, four years after the accident. There was a little girl named Mary who was so badly burned. Mary had no nose, her hair was not growing back, and she was permanently bald and had only a few fingers on her burned hands. But she had a smile–a *huge smile* on her face.

I spoke with her mother in the washroom. She had taken Mary to numerous healing seminars and was going to every one she could until Mary received her calling of God's healing touch.

> *Now faith is being sure of what we hope for and certain of what we do not see (Hebrews 11:1).*

Truth be known, I wanted to shake that mother. Did she not see Mary's smile, that huge smile? God was already doing a work in Mary, bringing her joy from the inside out!

Yeah, that is a good definition of faith. But the rest of the chapter lists miracle after miracle that God performed through the ancient of days. Read the rest of Hebrews 11 if you have time. It is amazing to see the miracles and the faith of God's people. However, it is even more amazing to see how God takes a seemingly negative situation and transforms it into a powerful turning point in life.

> *These were all commended for their faith, yet none of them received what had been promised. God had planned something better for us so that only together with us would they be made perfect (Hebrews 11:39–40).*

Christ is the resurrection and the light. We have immediate, instant triumph over our circumstances. Christ is the *something better* God had planned for you and me. My scars are on the outside; yours may be on the inside. We all have our issues, but with Jesus, our scars can be used as a powerful testimony for God.

When your life is saturated by the love of Christ, you are no longer visible to others. It is Christ who they see. I saw Mary's smile, and I saw Christ. He had already healed her. Her inside was beautiful; she was a walking testimony of God's love. Perfect!

Pour your heart out to God. Allow Him to saturate you with the love of Christ. Ask Him to make Himself visible to others through you.

Thoughts & Prayers

$\mathcal{D}ay\,26$

··

Valley of Despair

I n 1988, AIDS was on the rampage. The media was working hard to educate the public, and the public was nervous. I had not given it any thought. My lifestyle was not one that increased my chances of being infected by such a deadly disease. I was a church girl, a Bible student, and was living in my holy huddle. Not a problem.

But of course, it became a problem. The blood bank that donated blood to me in 1981 had given out contaminated blood. Those of us who had blood transfusions during that year needed to be checked out for AIDS. It was a five–day ordeal. My blood was drawn on Monday, and results were not given until Friday. This had to be the longest five days of my life! Every possible "What if" went through my mind.

Things were going so smoothly. I was in my third year of college, greatly anticipating graduation. I had met the man I knew I would marry. I was satisfied with my life's direction. Things could not possibly change so dramatically–yet again. I was on my knees pouring out my grievances to God. When I was not on my knees, my

119

mind was filled with negative thoughts as I educated myself on AIDS. It was a five–day journey through the valley of despair.

Have you been there? The valley of despair and the mountaintop of highs? "Lord, not another change!" The valley is dry, the grass is withered, and it is not the lush green of a meadow. There is no running water, no food. Where has the wild life gone? I am alone. I cry out for the hand of God to rescue me.

> *Turn your ear to me, come quickly to my rescue; be my rock of refuge, a strong fortress to save me (Psalms 31:2).*

Then I am reminded; You Lord are my rock, my strong fortress. It is in You where I find my strength. And so the journey begins. I start walking through the valley. My feet begin to heat up, and the thorns and stickers from the withered grass and weeds stick to my clothes. I am sweating profusely, and I need a drink of water.

> *But whoever drinks the water I give him will never thirst. Indeed, the water I give him will become in him a spring of water welling up to eternal life (John 4:14).*

That was You Jesus, encouraging my every step as I continue this journey. But my mind is so weak.

> *Look to the Lord and his strength; seek his face always. Remember the wonders he has done, his miracles, and the judgments he pronounced (1 Chronicles 16:11–12).*

The scenery has somehow changed, the air is cool, and there is a slight breeze. How refreshing to be on the mountaintop again. Friday came and so did the call from the blood bank. The news was good.

> *Jesus Christ is the same yesterday and today and forever (Hebrews 13:8).*

Have you been there? Have you made it through the valley where God sustains you and becomes your rock, your living water, and your strength? Have you made it to the mountaintop where you can rejoice and see that Jesus continues to be the same? Our circumstances can change within a single day, and yet for eternity, He remains the same.

Take time to reflect on those valleys and mountaintops where you have traveled. Write down your thoughts so next time, when you begin your journey, you will know He is faithful through the valley of despair all the way to the mountaintop.

Thoughts & Prayers

_____

_____

_____

_____

_____

_____

_____

_____

_____

_____

_____

_____

_____

_____

_____

_____

_____

_____

_____

_____

_____

_____

_____

_____

_____

_____

Enough is Enough

I have a difficult time making a fist with my right hand. Several tendons were severely damaged in the fire, resulting in limited use of my hand. A very delicate procedure of transferring tendons from one finger to the next would need to take place in order for me to be able to make a fist again. I have not done this procedure because it honestly does not matter to me.

A number of years after the accident, I did have a different type of surgery on my right hand. This procedure was to help the index finger and the thumb make a full circle when they touch. At the time, the two barely formed a teardrop. I was motivated to have this surgery because I wanted to be able to hold a cup.

Without the surgery, my hand was basically useless. With the surgery, I could envision being able to hold a pencil or being able to pick up a coin from the ground. Most of all, I wanted to be able to hold a can of Diet Pepsi. This alone was enough for me to accept going in for yet one more surgery. The surgery was a success, and I should have bought some stock in Pepsi with all of the cans this hand has now held.

It is very common for people to ask if I plan to have any more reconstructive surgery. And my reaction is, "Why should I?" God has given me a tool, an instant conversation piece. I am comfortable with who I am and how I look. As far as I am concerned, enough is enough. I just want to live life without surgeons.

I was burned by the fire, yet not consumed by it. Instead, the flames refined me. My scars are now my brand marks of Jesus Christ and my gateway to ministering to others who need to hear the Good News. God has given me a tool, and I will use it to bring honor and praise to Him.

> *Therefore, since we are receiving a kingdom that cannot be shaken, let us be thankful, and so worship God acceptably with reverence and awe, for our "God is a consuming fire" (Hebrews 12: 28–29).*

When will you let go and say, "Enough is enough?" When will you realize He has the best plan for you? He has a kingdom that cannot be shaken, and it is waiting for you.

What He has given you in this world is a tool meant to bring honor to Him. What is your tool that God has blessed you with? Identify it, write it down, and use it today! Worship Him and be thankful. Let the fire of God fill you, burn within you, and consume you. Give Him honor and praise!

Thoughts & Prayers

_____

_____

_____

_____

_____

_____

_____

_____

_____

_____

_____

_____

_____

_____

_____

_____

_____

_____

_____

_____

_____

_____

_____

_____

_____

Let the Children Come

C hildren are great at stating the obvious. "Your skin looks old!" "What happened to your skin? It looks weird!" When I explain that I was burned in a car accident, children always seem to come up with their own ideas as to the cause. "I know how it happened; there were bombs in the tires, right?" "Oh, I have seen on television how cars explode; was someone shooting at you?"

They usually have a story of a friend of a friend's cousin who got hurt in a car accident. After they share and are able to relate with me, they move on. Enough has been said. They are able to move on with their day. Adults, on the other hand, are not as well adjusted as children. They always seem to want to avoid the unknown–avoiding someone or something as if it does not exist.

At that time I was only dating my future husband Jim, and he was not sure about all of the looks, stares, and questions from little children. There was one incident when a small child was near us in a department store. The little boy had noticed my burns, but I did not see him. I was shopping, and my mind was elsewhere. But

Jim noticed the boy. "Mom, Mom! Did you see her skin? Mom, Mom! Why is her skin bloody?"

Apparently, it was obvious that this mother wanted to move her son quickly out of my audio range. Jim watched as her son continued to ask questions and his mother escorted him the opposite direction from us. The little child had questions; questions the mother could not answer.

If I had noticed this little boy, I would have answered his questions. We would have moved past this unknown and into something much deeper. We could have made a connection.

As adults, sometimes we get hung up on appearances. We are afraid to ask the hard questions. We avoid the unknown, because we are scared of confrontation. We live life with questions but not answers. Unfortunately, we all too often avoid the one source who has all of the answers.

> People were bringing little children to Jesus to have him touch them, but the disciples rebuked them. When Jesus saw this, he was indignant. He said to them, "Let the little children come to me, and do not hinder them, for the kingdom of God belongs to such as these. I tell you the truth, anyone who will not receive the kingdom of God like a little child will never enter it." And he took the children in his arms, put his hands on them and blessed them (Mark 10:13–16).

Move past appearances. Move past the unknown. Move into the arms of the source and into spiritual depth. Move into the One who can provide understanding. Be like the child and ask those hard questions. Let the One who can truly answer them connect with you. Ask God to reveal Himself to you and make that connection today.

Perhaps you need to share Christ with your friends. You may need to ask them the hard questions. Ask your friends if they know Jesus. Ask them if they would like to know the one source to answer their questions. By taking the initiative with your friends, by asking the hard questions as freely as a child, you will allow them to connect with God. Pray for that opportunity.

Thoughts & Prayers

_____
_____
_____
_____
_____
_____
_____
_____
_____
_____
_____
_____
_____
_____
_____
_____
_____
_____
_____
_____
_____
_____
_____

Day 29

* *

His Image

I was always a little insecure about my appearance. I would hide behind name brands; hoping people would notice the outfit and not the burns (or the extra five pounds that hung on my thighs). For a long time, wearing a swimsuit was unthinkable, especially in a public place.

For the first three years after my accident, the more fabric I had covering my skin the better I felt about myself. After the three years, I was beginning to adjust. I would wear three-quarter length pants and shirtsleeves. By the next summer, I decided that longer shorts and short sleeve T-shirts were more comfortable in the summer heat. But tank tops and mid-thigh shorts were out of the question for several more years.

After meeting Jim and dating him for a few years, my confidence was boosted. Eventually, I wore a swimsuit, but not in public–in my own hot tub. I figured that I had better show him the worst of it if I was serious about our relationship.

His acceptance brought me some peace. Slowly, I began to make public appearances in a swimsuit—but only within my comfort zone. If Jim and others who knew me were with me, I would go to the beach or the pool for short periods of time. But emotionally, this was draining and still can be.

For many years, I thought about appearances and self–esteem. Recently, I read a Christian book on self–image and I was greatly convicted. I was caught up in my own image, my own self–esteem. I was looking out for my own image when I should have been reflecting the image of God.

There is no self–image when Christ is your Savior. There is only the image of God. Remember, from the very beginning you were made in His image.

> *So God created man in his own image, in the image of God he created him; male and female he created them (Genesis 1:27).*

Let me ask you, where is your focus? Are you reflecting the image of God or are you projecting yourself and your own image? Be all that you were created to be. Reflect the image of God and be blessed.

Thoughts & Prayers

_____

_____

_____

_____

_____

_____

_____

_____

_____

_____

_____

_____

_____

_____

_____

_____

_____

_____

_____

_____

_____

_____

_____

_____

_____

_____

_____

Refreshed Hearts

Recently, I was challenged to take a second look at what God had done in my life. I had become comfortable–married with children. My testimony seemed insignificant–old news–nothing new on my resume. Why share my testimony when my plate was already overflowing? Was it not enough to raise a family of four boys? I thought so.

There I was, enjoying my vacation at a family camp where there were testimonies of Jesus' love walking everywhere. The week came to an end, and I had not shared my faith once. Others did and at least one man received the gift of eternal life. People were blessed and refreshed.

The people sharing their stories, of how Christ had changed their lives, experienced great joy as they saw how God was working in the lives of those around them. Somehow, I felt I had missed out on the blessing that others were experiencing as they rejoiced in the gift of salvation. They were exchanging hugs of encouragement while I stood back and watched. I longed to be a part of something that powerful.

Before I left camp that week, I expressed my thanks to one young man for sharing Christ. I also shared with him that God had used him to show me the importance of one's testimony. I needed to share how Christ had healed and worked in me.

At that point, it was amazing what God showed me. The young man lifted his pant legs to show me he was struggling with a skin disease called psoriasis. "You were a witness this week, even if you did not share a single word. I do not even wear shorts, and you put on a swimsuit. It spoke volumes to me," he said.

I really missed out! Sure I was thankful he saw me that way–a *witness*. But I felt like I lost a week of sharing, rejoicing, and encouraging others in Christ. The two of us had been given a tool, an instant conversation piece that can introduce others to Christ.

> *I pray that you may be active in sharing your faith, so that you will have a full understanding of every good thing we have in Christ. Your love has given me great joy and encouragement, because you, brother, have refreshed the hearts of the saints (Philemon 1:6–7).*

Why share your faith in Christ? Paul says it best when he explains how sharing one's faith will result in refreshed hearts. Do not underestimate God's work in you. Refresh the hearts of those around you. Share your story with others.

Thoughts & Prayers

From a Man's Perspective

I am not really sure what first attracted me to my wife, Wendi. I was a sixteen–year–old guy who had decided to freeload for an extra week at camp with my buddy, Mike. It was the last day of high school camp, and we were getting ready to pack our suitcases before the drive home.

Apparently, the camp director was desperate. He pulled Mike and me aside and asked us if we wanted to stay for an extra week for junior camp. He was short two guy counselors and needed help to handle the incoming fifth and sixth grade campers. Another week of meatloaf surprise and watery eggs; are you kidding me? God is good! So all the high school campers left, and Mike and I stayed.

Mike and I sat in the room anxiously awaiting our first official counselors' meeting. Soon, other camp counselors began to come in and take their seats. Two girls caught my attention right away. They looked exactly the same with brown hair, brown eyes, big smiles, and . . . burned skin. The scars caught me off guard. I had seen people with a small burn mark here or there, but never on half of their bodies. I soon found out that these two girl counselors were sisters and both had been burned in the same car accident just four years earlier. Wow, they must have really loved the camp food to put themselves in such a public and vulnerable environment.

As I got to know Wendi better that week, I found out it was not the food that she loved–it was Jesus. She knew she had been given a gift from God, and she wanted to share it with the campers. How cool was that?

There was one moment I will never forget. God decided to set up one of those divine appointments. All of the counselors were playing volleyball and Wendi and I were on the same team. Wendi was all over that volleyball court diving, spiking, jumping, laughing, and smiling. And then I saw it; she had Mary's smile. You remember the small burned child that Wendi described in Day 25–"Something Better?" Wendi had the same smile, the smile that truly reflected the beauty of her inner character. Her smile defined true love as it expressed her true love for Christ. Wendi's inner character was more beautiful than anyone I had ever met.

> A wife of noble character who can find? She is worth far more than rubies (Proverbs 31:10).

God had just slammed a two–by–four across my forehead, and my mind was spinning. At the time, I was on the football team and was dating an attractive, blonde cheerleader. Life was perfect. So why this divine intervention from God?

Starting at that moment, God began to teach me what true love really was. He showed me that love was not just a physical attraction, but rather a gift–the greatest gift from God. Through Wendi's smile and her deep brown eyes, I became blind to the scars and physical imperfections.

> But when perfection comes, the imperfect disappears (1 Corinthians 13:10).

He took a sixteen–year–old boy and took maturity to the next level. He showed me that physical appearances were not what mattered; rather it is the person's character that we need to fall in love with. What I realized was that Wendi's character, her faith in Christ, and her confidence in life were what attracted me to her. These were the attributes I desired in the person with whom I wanted to grow old.

> *Because we know that suffering produces perseverance; persever-*
> *ance, character; and character, hope. And hope does not disappoint*
> *us, because God has poured out his love into our hearts by the Holy*
> *Spirit, whom he has given us (Romans 5:3b–5).*

I often tell Wendi that, in our decade–plus of marriage, she has far exceeded all my expectations of a wife. Her character has evolved into something really special. The reason for this is that during her painful journey, she realized she had been given a gift from God and she chose to accept it. Wendi knew the only way she was go-ing to make it through that flaming storm was to accept God's peace and to use it as the ultimate prescription to survival.

Wendi was a diamond in the rough when I first met her. She was still recovering physically, emotionally, and spiritually from that fiery car crash just four years earlier. Today, I cannot thank God enough for putting that extra sparkle in her eyes and in her smile. The sparkle was what caught my attention, blinded me to physical imperfections, and opened my eyes to her inner beauty and her amazing character.

Wendi and I pray this devotional journey has both encouraged you and challenged you as you travel through your own flaming storm. Whether your scars are on the inside or on the outside, God's peace will guide you and protect you along your healing journey. You have been given a gift from God. Share it with others.

When you pass through the waters, I will be with you; and when you pass through the rivers, they will not sweep over you. When you walk through the fire, you will not be burned; the flames will not set you ablaze (Isaiah 43:2).

Thoughts & Prayers

_____
_____
_____
_____
_____
_____
_____
_____
_____
_____
_____
_____
_____
_____
_____
_____
_____
_____
_____
_____
_____
_____
_____
_____
_____
_____
_____
_____

Index

a

Acceptance – Day 27
Anger – Day 24
Anxiety – Day 18

c

Change – Day 9
Character – Day 31
Comfort – Day 17, 26
Contentment – Day 25
Control – Day 2, 24
Cure – Day 2

e

Endurance – Day 4

f

Faith – Day 25
Fear – Day 18, 19, 20
Friendship – Day 15
Frustration – Day 16

g

Goals – Day 15
Grace – Day 12

h

Healing – Day 3, 5, 11
Hiding – Day 20
Hope – Day 7, 9

i

Identity – Day 22
Isolation – Day 11

j

Journey – Day 26
Joy – Day 25

k

Listening – Day 10
Love – Day 31

m

Mercy – Day 12

n

Nourishment – Day 6, 16

p

Pain – Day 3, 4
Peace – Day 1, 2
Perseverance – Day 3
Prayer – Day 11

r

Reality –Day 8
Renewal – Day 13, 23

s

Scripture – Day 6, 17, 26
Self–image – Day 29
Selfishness – Day 14
Sharing – Day 30
Sin – Day 21, 22
Strength – Day 8

t

Testimony – Day 23, 30
Therapy – Day 17
Transforming – Day 23

u

Understanding – Day 28

v

Vision – Day 3, 15

w

Witnessing – Day 23

To order additional copies of

PEACE
in a FLAMING
STORM

Please call:

1–877–421–READ (7323)

or please visit our web site at
www.pleasantword.com

Also available at: www.amazon.com

Printed in the United States
25377LVS00004B/319-378